YOUR KNOWLEDGE HAS VALUE

- We will publish your bachelor's and master's thesis, essays and papers

- Your own eBook and book - sold worldwide in all relevant shops

- Earn money with each sale

Upload your text at www.GRIN.com
and publish for free

Bibliographic information published by the German National Library:

The German National Library lists this publication in the National Bibliography; detailed bibliographic data are available on the Internet at http://dnb.dnb.de .

This book is copyright material and must not be copied, reproduced, transferred, distributed, leased, licensed or publicly performed or used in any way except as specifically permitted in writing by the publishers, as allowed under the terms and conditions under which it was purchased or as strictly permitted by applicable copyright law. Any unauthorized distribution or use of this text may be a direct infringement of the author s and publisher s rights and those responsible may be liable in law accordingly.

Imprint:

Copyright © 2015 GRIN Verlag
Print and binding: Books on Demand GmbH, Norderstedt Germany
ISBN: 9783668682184

This book at GRIN:

https://www.grin.com/document/416991

Abbe Marten

Maintaining The Balance. Public Safety vs. Social Justice and Environmental Protection vs. Economic Expansion

GRIN Verlag

GRIN - Your knowledge has value

Since its foundation in 1998, GRIN has specialized in publishing academic texts by students, college teachers and other academics as e-book and printed book. The website www.grin.com is an ideal platform for presenting term papers, final papers, scientific essays, dissertations and specialist books.

Visit us on the internet:

http://www.grin.com/

http://www.facebook.com/grincom

http://www.twitter.com/grin_com

Union County College

Maintaining the Balance

Public Safety vs. Social Justice and Environmental Protection vs. Economic Expansion

Abbe Allen

Introduction to Urban Studies

23 March 2015

From the beginning of the colonization of American to the urban unit of today, citizens of the United States how struggled with the concept of how best to organize the country in such a way so as to minimize costs while also expanding the economy and allowing growth. Attempts to achieve a balance between public safety and social justice as well as between environmental preservation and economic development have always fallen short in the past but there is hope that by the year 2050, the United States can be made over into an image of social and environmental justice that nurtures the quality of life in this country while balancing spending and the economy. Restorative justice and community justice are recently proposed methods for the reform of the justice system, utilizing community engagement to create change and deter crime. To further improve upon the urban unit is the idea of sustainability, which seeks to promote environmental justice with more efficient building standards and the facilitation of community life. With the combination of these two ideas, there is a hope that the United States can revitalize the norm of the urban unit, making it not only cost-effective, but able to serve the people in a better way.

Today's legal system is ill equipped to adequately manage the discrimination that is embedded into all aspects of justic. There are too many opportunities for officials in the legal system to corrupt the adjudication process under the stealth of authority, it is only with reformulating these practices and policies with community involvement that social justice can be achieved in conjunction with the goal of public safety. Restorative justice emphasizes repairing the harm caused or revealed by crime through a cooperative process involving all stakeholders. It redefines the traditional relationship between communities and their government in responding to crime by using new programs that are categorized by four values: encounter, amends, reintegration, and inclusion. The victim, offender, and members of the community are allowed the opportunity to *encounter* one another through victim-offender mediation, family/community group conferencing, and sanctioning circles. The *restitution* is then agreed in the appropriate forum, favoring community service over incarceration so that they offender can make *amends* for the crime committed. Community members and social service agencies supervise the restitution process while offering support to facilitate reintegration of the offender while while simultaneously providing support to facilitate *his* inclusion in the community.

Victim-offender mediation is currently the most widespread restorative justice practice. In this model, offenders and victims meet with volunteer mediators to discuss the effect of the crime committed, their feelings and concerns, and to work out a restitution agreement. The primary goal is the safety of the community and personal growth wherein the restitution is secondary. It is believed that by developing an offender's empathy for the victim, there is a decrease in recidivism and when the victim is able to speak with the offender face-to-face, there is justice. This method is widely used in many countries such as Austria where it became an official part of the juvenile justice system in 1989. In practice, victim-offender mediation has proven successful for juvenile and adult petty crimes and arguably in more serious and even violent crimes on a case-by-case basis as proved in the legal system of British Colombia. Family group conferencing is based on the same rationale as victim-offender mediation, however it involves a broader range of people (family, friends, peers, coworkers) that are utilized to take collective responsibility for the offender carrying out his restitution. This ensures that the offender is held accountable for his actions while also tapping into the capacity of non-governmental (community-based) organizations to handle related public safety issues. This has been successful in Australia when it was founded in the 1990's, with family group conferencing being adopted in every state and territory, with community members taking on the tasks of the juvenile justice system completely in 1998. Sentencing circles may have some limited use as well in the restorative justice theory as shown in its' practice in some inner-city black communities in Minnesota. These circles are open to the public as well as the victim and offender so that citizens can express their concerns about the crimes committed and provide support for both the victim and offender. These methods: victim-offender mediation, family group conferencing, and sentencing circles; allow the victim to take an active role in the justice process and allows the offender to be socialized so as to replace his criminal ties with healthier social ties. Offenders in these restorative programs are more likely to complete the restitution program and are much less likely to re-offend because they understand their impact and have the reintegration services necessary to develop the skills to contribute to society.

Through the use of restorative probation and other citizen boards in place of traditional incarceration, probation, and other monitoring systems; cases can be taken on in a community setting at a faster pace with little preparation. In places where restorative probation is practiced such as in Vermont, a judge defers his probation decision to volunteer citizens of the Reparative Citizen Board whom draft an agreement for reparations and associated probation. This use has shown a great deal of promise in juvenile and minor offense cases such as drug possession and shoplifting. In the places where these types of community-based programs are used, there has been little problem with getting citizens to volunteer and the needs of the processes are adequately met with appropriate managerial supervision. Utilizing different sanctioning policies in place of incarceration such as community service, drug treatment, education, and reintegration of the offender, the community as a whole can benefit from the legal system and crimes can be thwarted. When sanctions and mediation occur by one's peers, satisfaction is greatly increased because the best people to meet the needs of the society are these peers themselves. Residents report that the system is more just than the traditional system due to the individualization in its' practice; citizens take control of the process of restitution and there is little opportunity for discrimination and corruption done under the guise of authority. When the reparative process simply imposes proportional costs to the offenders for the harm they have wrought instead of rehabilitation and reintegration, 75% of them are arrested again within five years. Through the use of restorative justice programs however, this statistic has been slashed in half.

Similar to restorative justice, community justice seeks to build a partenrship between government agencies and the affected community through the inclusion of the common citizen. Although still largely only a theory, this idea ideally consists of loosely related, innovative projects and programs that operate at the community level. Both restorative and community justice share a concern for the victims, prioritizing reparations and amends over imprisonment punishments and associated fines. When justice is served on a neighborhood level, each community can be individualized in their practices. It is assumed that all citizens: offender, victim, and otherwise, have an obligation to the community based solely on their residence in it and therefore must be expected to take responsibility for public safety. Volunteerism may allow for some governmental agencies to be combined and some positions within them to be matrixed, facilitating the improvement of coordination and cross-fertilization of ideas. Compacting the necessary government agencies involved in the justice system considerably decreases state and federal spending for staffing, offices, and day-to-day budgets. Community justice is rooted in the idea that the U.S. is a democratic nation, and all citizens therefore have a duty to become involved in the community. This proposal provides citizens opportunities to practice this democracy by fulfilling such duties as providing support to crime victims, assisting offenders in reintegration back into community, and carrying out community crime prevention activities. With these services operating at a local level, communities can become self-regulating and further reinforce legal norms and laws to decrease crime and encourage responsibility.

Community justice seeks to utilize four main processes in order to achieve its' ideal: system accessibility, community involvement, reparative processes, and re-integrative processes. By facilitating greater accessibility to services through the informality of such methods as foot patrols, citizen surveys, resident-driven search warrants, and victim-offender mediation; community involvement is encouraged due to the inherent ease of access in these methods. Operationally, community justice means thinking in terms of blocks of space instead of cities, counties, and states. Criminal justice activities will be tied to these localities and will be free to adapt to the individuality of community life there. The geospecific information generated based on these blocks of space help to organize the localities into priorities so that high-crime areas can receive greater attention and greater investment of state and federal resources. Budget money can thereby be delegated to those areas most in need so as to facilitate the most efficient spending. The prominence of de jure segregation in most neighborhoods allows members of the community to be policed and mediated by their peers who may be of the same race and upbringing which serves to reduce discrimination based on age, race, and sex within the community. The traditional legal system has a very low satisfaction rating, but in places where community justice is used like New York City's Midtown Community Court, these satisfaction ratings prove to increase significantly. When peers are determining appropriate restitution requirements for offenders and aid in support of the victim, the justice system is unbiased and fair to all involved. Community justice devolves the decision-making process while empowers residents and encouraging active participation in maintaing public safety.

The physical atmosphere of a community may be related to its' crime rate as was proven in the renovation of New York City's Bryant Park, when beautification projects transformed it from an open-air drug market to a family-friendly atmosphere. Through simple additions such as increased lighting, better visibility, and planting greenery, crime can be prevented adverted and public safety can be fostered. These beautifcation projects serve to make urban units more equitable, healthy, and sustainable; while simultaneously serving environmental justice.

In the environmental justice movement, the uneven distribution of toxic, hazardous waste facilities is addressed through community engagement in planning and land use decision thereby promoting public health and strengthening existing communities. Trees and flowers are just part of a bigger sceme that involves making priorities that balance economic preservation and economic expansion. The key to prosperity in the United States is learning to set these prioritis wisely, at any one time we have unlimited wants and needs but only a limited amount of resources for achieving them. Firms and consumers are not paying the full costs of their actions, dishonestly burdening taxpayers with the costs and future generations and their governments with the long-term environmental consequences. In order to ensure that those who profit from the destruction of the environment immediately pays for it, the economic "Hartwick rule" theory mandates that a percentage of the profits from using non-renewable resources such as oil and minerals be invested in alternative market assets in order to ensure a sustainable environment and economy. The bulk of environmental protection depends on the development of technology to reduce pollution of water, toxic waste, and emissions which leaves the question of what to do in the mean time. After priorities are set, what else can we do besides wait? The most viable proposal is in investing in the sustainable preservation of existing buildings and resources, implementing green practices to strengthen these existing communities instead of continuing urban sprawl.

Meaningful community engagement in planning and land use decisions is the beginning to ensuring broad support for green proposal projects and effective public processes. Through the use of multilingual outreach to get more community members involved; residents can help gather, analyze, and report information about current conditions and needs related to priority issues in their neighborhoods. Federal, state, and local regional planners can hold community planning and visioning workshops to define a shared vision and goals for the neighborhood, thereby laying a foundation for subsequent land use policy and regulatory changes and investments. By designing neighborhoods and buildings to protect air, water, land, and public health; future pollution can be avoided, the rate of disease can be decreased, and quality of life can be increased. Proactive cooperation among community residents, all levels of government, and business and industry stakeholders is imperative when planning these rennovations. Multi-stakehoolder collaboration during the planning stage allows early identification of potential negative impacts so that municipal planners can work with state and local environmental air, and transportation agencies to understand expected environmental problems. These environmental agencies should become involved in the planning, zoning, and permitting tools can be processes when planning proposed facilities so as to do so safely and to reduce residents' exposure to environmentally dangerous facilities. Existing facilities can be utilized, cleaning and reusing contaminated properties for commercial and industrial activities, housing, parks, and other community facilities. Money must be spent wisely in the expansion of urban sprawl, but by rennovating existing infrastructures instead of building completely new developments, each dollar spent on construction gives a surplus of job opportunities that can contribute to the economy long after the completion of the project. To further prioritze money spent, communities should look at the picture as a whole instead of individual sites in order to better identify the most productive and appropriate reuse options. By ammending existing policies that complicate the reconstruction and reuse process and providing education to the community at large, private entities are compelled to invest in their neighborhoods and facilitate the renovation of abandoned buildings into community attractions that offer residents accessible jobs, services, and amenities.

    Green buildings use sustainable siting, design, and materials to create a healthy community and environment. When operated appropriately, green buildings can reduce exposure to toxins and pollutants by including natural landscaping features to capture and filter polluted runoff that would otherwise infest local bodies of water. A "fix-it-first strategy should be implemented prioritizing the maintainence and repair of existing infrastructures over the construction of new ones in undeveloped places. Public investment in infrastructure maintenance shows commitment to the community and thereby encourages private sectors to invest in these renovations. Necessary roadway repair and maintenance, and mixeuse, compact development projects create more jobs per dollar than building a new infrastructure. If there are no available existing structures to use, new buildings can be constructed with further opportunities to make the city green. Builders participating work with certified experts to incorporate features such as insulation, high-performance windows, efficient heating systems, and efficient cooling systems to save costs and reduce harmful impacts to the environment. The requirement of adherence to these efficiency standards in the creation of all new buildings and as appropriate, in the renovation of existing buildings, can reduce our impact on the environment by 20-30%. Moreover, by incorporating greenery into construction plans and renovating the streets and community property around them, green streets can be developed that reinforce environmental justice. The plants and soils used in the gardens, medians, and planters of facilities constructed help to filter and break down pollutants while trees catch and absorb rainfall to help water evaporation and porous materials. When there is available budget money, concrete and asphalt can be replaced with porous materials to improve air quality by reducing the "heat islands" the occur when concrete are heated in the Summer.

    The United States is riddled with run-down strip malls and vacant gas stations that have promise for redevelopment as safe, convenient, and vibrant thoroughfares. By renovating these properties, commercial corridors can enhance the customer base of the existing businesses, create new jobs and business opportunities for residents, and improve the safety and convenience of transportation options. Local governments can use pedestrian-friendly land use patterns and zoning tools such as mixed-use ordinances that put homes and workplaces close together. Municipalities can make streets safer for pedestrians with narrower traffic lanes to slow traffic while benefiting businesses by allowing for on-street parking to attract spending. Public investment along commercial corridor through sidewalk improvements, lighting, trees, greenery, and other basic amenities can draw additional public, private, and nonprofit investments into the community. By building relationships with business owners and giving grants for commercial corridor improvements, local government can promote revitalization. One example of the successful use of corridor revitalization on a large scale is in the Grand Boulevard Initiative wherein a collection of 19 cities, counties, regional agencies, businesses, labor groups, and developers worked together to improve California's El Camiro Real, the 600-mile historic highway. As shown in this example, through the facilitation of local partnerships, revitalization attempts can, with proper organization and planning, radiate to larger districts thereby improving private funding sources to alleviate the financial burden of these renovations.

Public transit, bicycle, and pedestrian networks are critical links to the regional employment and educational opportunities for those in low-income and overburdened communities that are affected the most by toxic wastes and contaminated buildings. Expanding public transportation options and redesigning streets to be safe for pedestrian use reduces the need for personal vehicles and their plethora of pollution which would naturally improve air quality, environmental dangers, and some illnesses such as asthma. Planning land use so that homes, businesses, and civic buildings are located near public transit and translating schedules and brochures into local languages improves accessibility so as to facilitate contribution to the community and further invigorating the economy. In places such as La Jolla Band of Luiseno Indians in southern California, officials are using other cost-efficient strategies to promote this necessary accessibility and safety such as marking stops more clearly, calming traffic, and protecting the roadside paths the lead to the stops from vehicles using logs and other natural barriers obtained from the surrounding landscape. Those community members that use these public services need to play a hand in the planning and construction of them as in Settle, where a citizen transportation advisory committee was formed to advise the mayor and city council on transportation priorities. Representatives from diverse communities conduct assessments to uncover specific transportation needs so as to best design the transit system, who better to voice their needs than the people themselves?

Some of these abandoned buildings should be renovated into community-centered schools located near the families it serves, accessible via multiple modes of transportation, and leaving a very small footprint. Because community-centered schools are centrally located, students, parents, and faculty can access the services and jobs available, thereby reducing barriers to education. Without an adequate education, citizens are unable to adequately contribute to society and may resort to criminal pursuits to fund their lifestyle. The greater accessibility of education and related jobs provides purpose for residents from 9-3 while after hours can be used for broader community use through the partnership with the city recreation department and other governmental agencies. The resources of the school including the kitchen, classrooms, library, and gardens provide ample opportunity for adult classes, boy scout meetings, voting, and more. Economic research shows that low-income neighborhoods can have significant purchasing power and unmet demand. There is possibility for economic expansion, however there is little opportunity for these residents to become involved in the consumer culture. Through the creation of local schools, jobs can be created and surrounding businesses can expand to revitalize the community.

Green space is one of the most cost-effective and most influential ways to create sustainable communities. Parks, community gardens, playing fields, and shorelines offer opportunities for residents to engage in physical activity and social engagement while providing a habitat for wildlife and serving important biological functions such as lowering ambient temperatures and absorbing rainwater to reduce flooding. The Bootheel Heart Health Project in Missouri built walking trails in rural, predominantly African-American communities and found that almost 60% of trail users reported more community involvement as a result of the accessibility of trails. Some places such as the Olneyville Housing Corporation in Providence, Rhode Island utilize a partnership with police officials so as the redesign these green spaces to serve the dual use of crime prevention. As a result of this planning, this area of Providence transitioned from one of the most dangerous parts of the city to a well-used family attraction. By involving community members in the construction of trails and other landscape projects, costs can be reduced as the burden of governmental officials is dispersed. Governmental officials and individuals of vastly different aspects of the community such as police officers, environmental experts, advocates, mediators, construction companies, and politicians can unite to strengthen the urban unit, preserve the environment, protect public safety, serve social justice, and act as a catalyst for the economy in a broader global scope by the year 2050. It's time to provide opportunities for average citizens to contribute to their communities; we, as U.S. citizens savor the freedom of the democracy we live in, but with this democracy comes great responsibility and the time to take on that burden is now.

Works Cited

Adler School. "White Paper on Restorative Justice: A Primer and Exploration of Practice Across Two North American Cities." Adler School on Public Safety and Social Justice and Illinois Coalition for Immigrant and Refugee Rights, 2012. Web 27 Mar. 2015. <https://www.adler.edu/resources/content/4/1/documents/RJ_WhitePaper_Final_13_04_29.pdf>

Chudacoff, Howard P. *The Evolution of American Urban Society.* 7th ed. Upper Saddle River: Prentice-Hall, 2010. 215-281. Print.

McConville, Megan. "Creating Equitable, Healthy, and Sustainable Communities: Strategies for Advancing Smart Growth, Environmental Justice, and Equitable Development." *EPA*. U.S. Environmental Protection Agency, Feb. 2013. Web. 27 Mar. 2015. <http://www.epa.gov/smartgrowth/pdf/equitable-dev/equitable-development-report-508-011713b.pdf>.

McKitrik, Ross. "Choosing Priorities to Balance Economic Growth and Environmental Protection." 2011. Web. 27 Mar. 2015. <http://www.rossmckitrick.com/uploads/4/8/0/8/4808045/ beijing_forum_mckitrick.pdf>.

Karp, David, and Todd Clear. "Community Justice: A Conceptual Framework." Boundary Changes in Criminal Justice Organizations. Skidmore College, 2000. Web. 27 Mar. 2015. <https://www.skidmore.edu/campuslife/karp/book-chapters/Community-Justice-A-Conceptual-Framework.pdf>.

Kurki, Leena. "Incorporation Restorative and Community Justice Into American Sentencing and Corrections." *Sentencing & Corrections: Issues for the 21st Century.* National Institute of Justice, Sept. 1999. Web. 27 Mar. 2015. <https://www.ncjrs.gov/pdffiles1/nij/175723.pdf>.

YOUR KNOWLEDGE HAS VALUE

- We will publish your bachelor's and master's thesis, essays and papers

- Your own eBook and book - sold worldwide in all relevant shops

- Earn money with each sale

Upload your text at www.GRIN.com
and publish for free